CYBER THREATS

DISINFORMATION CAMPAIGNS

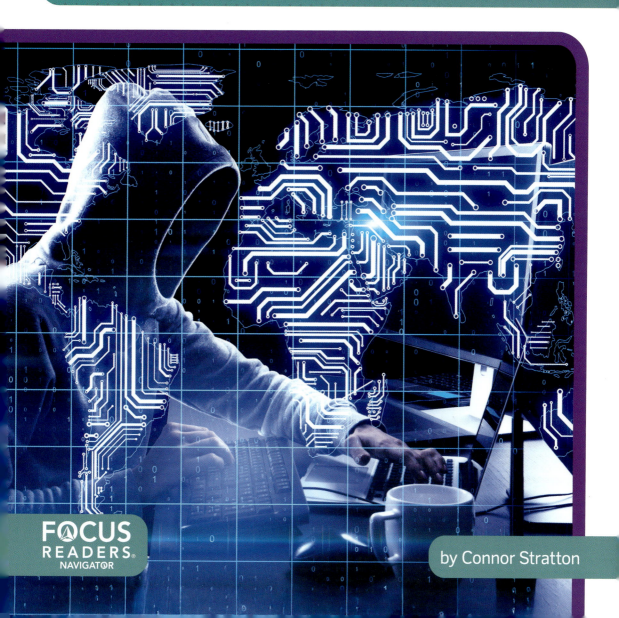

by Connor Stratton

WWW.FOCUSREADERS.COM

Copyright © 2026 by Focus Readers®, Mendota Heights, MN 55120. All rights reserved. No part of this book may be reproduced or utilized in any form or by any means without written permission from the publisher.

Focus Readers is distributed by North Star Editions:
sales@northstareditions.com | 888-417-0195

Produced for Focus Readers by Red Line Editorial.

Photographs ©: Shutterstock Images, cover, 1, 7, 8–9, 11, 14–15, 17, 19, 20–21, 23, 25, 26, 29; Democracy News Alliance/news aktuell/AP Images, 4–5; Red Line Editorial, 13

Library of Congress Cataloging-in-Publication Data
Names: Stratton, Connor, author.
Title: Disinformation campaigns / by Connor Stratton.
Description: Mendota Heights, MN: Focus Readers, [2026] | Series: Cyber threats | Includes index. | Audience term: Children | Audience: Grades 4-6
Identifiers: LCCN 2024059380 (print) | LCCN 2024059381 (ebook) | ISBN 9798889985174 (hardcover) | ISBN 9798889985785 (pdf) | ISBN 9798889985495 (ebook)
Subjects: LCSH: Disinformation--Juvenile literature. | Media literacy--Juvenile literature.
Classification: LCC HM1231 .S848 2026 (print) | LCC HM1231 (ebook) | DDC 302.23--dc23/eng/20250115
LC record available at https://lccn.loc.gov/2024059380
LC ebook record available at https://lccn.loc.gov/2024059381

Printed in the United States of America
Mankato, MN
082025

ABOUT THE AUTHOR
Connor Stratton writes and edits nonfiction children's books. He lives in Minnesota.

TABLE OF CONTENTS

CHAPTER 1
The 2024 Presidential Election 5

CHAPTER 2
How It Works 9

CHAPTER 3
Purpose and Impact 15

CHAPTER 4
Fighting Disinformation 21

CYBER SAFETY
Media Literacy 28

Focus Questions • 30
Glossary • 31
To Learn More • 32
Index • 32

CHAPTER 1

THE 2024 PRESIDENTIAL ELECTION

In November 2024, Americans voted for a new president. Vice President Kamala Harris was running. So was former president Donald Trump.

Leading up to November, voters heard a lot about the election. Candidates spent billions of dollars on TV and online ads. Thousands of reporters covered Harris

In September 2024, Kamala Harris and Donald Trump took part in a televised debate.

and Trump. And millions of people shared election content on social media.

However, not all of this content was true. In fact, some of the information was false on purpose. This is known as disinformation. Much of it came from Americans. But some disinformation came from other countries.

For example, some disinformation came from Russia. The US government charged two Russian people with crimes. Lawyers said they secretly paid a US media company. Then the company's **influencers** spread false, pro-Russia information. The influencers' videos racked up millions of views on YouTube.

In 2024, Russian disinformation videos also spread on social media sites such as X.

In the end, the result of the 2024 election was clear. Trump was elected the 47th president of the United States. The impact that disinformation had on the result was uncertain. But disinformation remained an important issue.

CHAPTER 2

HOW IT WORKS

Every day, people come across information about the world around them. Sometimes this information is false. False information comes in two types. The first kind is misinformation. That happens when people accidentally spread falsehoods. For example, a person may read a news article and

▶ Some people get daily news from reading newspapers. Others find news online.

misremember a few details. Then they share wrong information.

The second type of false information is disinformation. It often comes through disinformation campaigns. That's when groups of people work together. They spread false information on purpose.

Disinformation campaigns are not new. People have used them for thousands of years. It even happened in ancient Rome. In one instance, two different Roman leaders competed for power. The leaders spread lies about one another. Each hoped to ruin the other person's chances.

Disinformation has changed over time. New technology has made it easier to

In the early 2020s, TikTok had more than one billion users.

spread. The internet is a key part of that. For example, people can create websites with fake information. They can make false posts on social media. Billions of people use those sites.

Many disinformation campaigns use troll farms. That's when people pay others to spread disinformation online. The paid trolls post false or **divisive** content.

Artificial intelligence (AI) also helps spread disinformation. People can use AI to create false content that seems real. For example, AI can help **bot accounts** seem like real users. That makes their content more believable.

DEEPFAKES

Some people use AI to make deepfakes. A deepfake can be an image, video, or piece of audio. For example, some people make deepfakes of political leaders. AI videos may show a leader saying something horrible. The leader never said it. However, the deepfakes make people believe the leader did. As a result, citizens might get angry at that leader. Deepfakes can make disinformation more powerful.

Some disinformation does not reach far. Other times, it spreads widely. Big influencers may post it. News reports may mention false information. Even trusted leaders may repeat false claims.

HOW DISINFORMATION SPREADS QUICKLY

Each person can spread disinformation to many others.

CHAPTER 3

PURPOSE AND IMPACT

People use disinformation campaigns for several purposes. They often play a role during elections. Groups may spread false claims about a candidate. Some disinformation campaigns make voters angry at a candidate. Voters may be more likely to choose the opponent.

> Disinformation can cause people to doubt the voting process.

Sometimes governments use disinformation. Some may even use it against their own citizens. For instance, leaders may want to stop criticisms. Turkey's government is one example.

FACEBOOK IN MYANMAR

In 2017, Myanmar's military carried out disinformation. It targeted the country's Rohingya people. The military set up Facebook accounts. The accounts spread false, hateful disinformation about the Rohingya and Islam. Facebook's **algorithm** helped spread the hate speech. Violence followed. Soldiers and others killed many Rohingya people. They destroyed hundreds of villages. Hundreds of thousands of Rohingya people fled the country.

The British Petroleum Company spread disinformation about climate change in the past. In 1997, the company began changing its actions.

In the 2020s, it used bots and troll farms on social media. The fake accounts praised Turkey's government.

Greed can also drive disinformation campaigns. For example, fossil fuel companies sometimes spread disinformation. Burning fossil fuels such as oil and gas adds to **climate change**. Many people want to address

17

this crisis. They think people should limit the use of fossil fuels. However, fossil fuel companies don't like that idea. They would lose money. So, some companies take action. They cast doubt on climate change and its solutions. They try to delay changes.

In 2020, COVID-19 spread across the world. This disease killed millions. It also disrupted many people's lives. People felt fear and confusion. They wanted answers and treatments. But it took time for scientists to develop a vaccine. This crisis became a chance for disinformation. Some groups spread false claims about real treatments. These groups said their

COVID-19 vaccines were approved in 2021. However, disinformation led many people to distrust the vaccines.

products could cure COVID-19. That led people to buy their products.

Over time, disinformation can have a wider impact. For example, people may lose trust in other people or news sources. That can cause people to reject new information. When that happens, bringing people together and sharing information becomes difficult.

CHAPTER 4

FIGHTING DISINFORMATION

People can help fight disinformation campaigns. Fact-checking is one common method. Some fact-checkers work for news sources. Some websites also focus on fact-checking. Other times, social media users can fact-check posts. When a claim spreads widely, fact-checkers step in. They research the

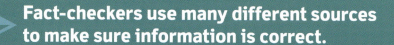

Fact-checkers use many different sources to make sure information is correct.

claim. Then they say whether it is true or not.

Fact-checking can help **debunk** false claims. But it has limits. For example, fact-checking usually addresses false claims one by one. It may not look for larger patterns. So, it may not spot wider disinformation campaigns. Fact-checking also happens after claims have already spread. People may see the false claims but never see the fact-checks. Or they may not believe the fact-checks.

For this reason, some groups try to get ahead of disinformation. This method is sometimes called "pre-bunking." For example, some officials prepare

In 2022, Arizona officials released a pre-bunking video. It explained why it takes time to count election ballots.

for false claims before elections. They expect false claims about **voter fraud** to spread. So, officials put out information well before the vote. They explain what disinformation people might see. When people encounter it, they are ready. They can question the claims.

Other steps can stop disinformation from spreading as widely. Tech companies play a key role. They control platforms where lots of information spreads. Companies can use tools to

YOUTUBE RULES

The 2020 US presidential election was not impacted by voter fraud. However, false claims about that issue were common. In response, YouTube changed its rules. It removed videos that claimed voter fraud had changed the 2020 election. It also banned accounts that kept breaking this rule. The changes worked. Election disinformation dropped on YouTube. However, YouTube weakened these rules in 2023. Disinformation rose again.

In 2022, the European Union adopted the Digital Services Act. The act aims to reduce the spread of disinformation online.

find bots, troll farms, and deepfakes. Then companies can remove those accounts. Companies may also adjust their algorithms. They can make false content less likely to spread. And they can make truthful content easier to spread.

Schools can teach students ways to watch out for disinformation.

Governments play a role as well. They can create laws against disinformation. For instance, countries in Europe took action in the 2020s. Lawmakers made rules for tech companies. Companies could face fines if they allowed disinformation to spread.

Improving local media can help, too. In the United States, fewer towns have their own newspapers than in the past. So, people often turn to social media for news. Disinformation spreads easily on those sites. More local news with strong fact-checking could slow the spread.

Improving media literacy is another tool. Media literacy is about how people think about information. It involves reading news and other information with a sharp eye. People with high media literacy can think critically. They can figure out whether or not information is reliable. If more people have those skills, disinformation becomes less effective.

CYBER SAFETY

MEDIA LITERACY

Everyone can learn media literacy. First, people should pause after coming across a claim. Is the statement claiming to be fact? If so, more research can reveal if it is really true.

People should look up the source of the claim. Does the author have a trustworthy background for the topic? Next, research should focus on the claim itself. People may look up other sources about the topic. Do those sources say something similar? Learning the original **context** of the claim is important.

Not all online images and videos are real. So, people should carefully study images and videos. Small details may offer clues. For example, many deepfakes swap out faces. Does the face's skin match the body's skin? Do the lips move along with the words? Spotting those things can help identify disinformation.

In the 2020s, technology that people use to make deepfakes became available more widely.

AI is always improving. Sometimes it is not easy to tell real from fake. If something online seems strange, asking a trusted adult can help. Also, people should never share something until they know it's true. That way, they won't spread disinformation.

FOCUS QUESTIONS

Write your answers on a separate piece of paper.

1. Write a paragraph explaining the main ideas of Chapter 4.

2. Where do you get most of your information? How do you know whether the information is trustworthy?

3. What is misinformation?
    - A. true information that people do not believe
    - B. a government-run effort to spread false information
    - C. the spread of false information by mistake

4. Why did disinformation rise after YouTube weakened its rules in 2023?
    - A. The weaker rules let more videos with untrue facts be viewed and posted.
    - B. The weaker rules stopped as many videos with untrue facts from being viewed and posted.
    - C. The weaker rules made people stop watching videos on YouTube.

Answer key on page 32.

GLOSSARY

algorithm
A set of rules that decide what content is shown to users online.

artificial intelligence
The ability of a machine to make decisions on its own.

bot accounts
Online accounts run by AI that aim to seem like real people.

climate change
A human-caused global crisis involving long-term changes in Earth's temperature and weather patterns.

context
The words, phrases, and information that surround a piece of a text and help people understand what it means.

debunk
To show that a claim is false.

divisive
Likely to cause disagreements.

influencers
People who use social media to make many people interested in something.

voter fraud
The crime of trying to affect the result of an election through illegal voting methods.

TO LEARN MORE

BOOKS

Carser, A. R. *What Is Fake News?* BrightPoint Press, 2023.
Gatling, Alex. *Fake News in Focus*. Focus Readers, 2022.
Kuehl, Ashley. *Deepfakes*. Bearport Publishing, 2025.

NOTE TO EDUCATORS

Visit **www.focusreaders.com** to find lesson plans, activities, links, and other resources related to this title.

INDEX

algorithms, 16, 25
artificial intelligence (AI), 12, 29

bot accounts, 12, 17, 25

climate change, 17–18
COVID-19, 18–19

deepfakes, 12, 25, 28

elections, 5–7, 15, 23–24

Facebook, 16
fact-checking, 21–22, 27

internet, 11

leaders, 10, 12–13, 16

media literacy, 27, 28
misinformation, 9

Russia, 6

social media, 6, 11, 17, 21, 27

tech companies, 24, 26
trolls, 11, 17, 25

United States, 6–7, 24, 27

voter fraud, 23–24

YouTube, 6, 24

Answer Key: 1. Answers will vary; 2. Answers will vary; 3. C; 4. A